A Book of Lyrics
from the Album

We'll Get Through

PATRICIA REYNOLDS
and JAMES DUNN

Photography by PAUL GANA

tate publishing
AND ENTERPRISES, LLC

Published by Tate Publishing & Enterprises, LLC
127 E. Trade Center Terrace | Mustang, Oklahoma 73064 USA
1.888.361.9473 | www.tatepublishing.com

Tate Publishing is committed to excellence in the publishing industry. The company reflects the philosophy established by the founders, based on Psalm 68:11,
"The Lord gave the word and great was the company of those who published it."

Book design copyright © 2014 by Tate Publishing, LLC. All rights reserved.
Cover and interior design by Errol Villamante
Photos by Paul Gana

Published in the United States of America

ISBN: 978-1-63185-574-0
1. Music / Lyrics
2. Music / Reference
14.08.08

Artists' Biography

Pat Reynolds and Jim Dunn met in 2006, at a cafe in Indian Lake, New York, where Pat was helping out part-time. Soon after, at a New Year's Party, she encountered Jim's wonderful voice, as he was singing a karaoke song. She invited him to join a music group she had been a member of for years, and they have been singing together ever since. Pat, a mother of five and grandmother of ten, had previously written and recorded two songs in Nashville in 1996, when she gained the attention of  Robert Metzgar after performing a song on the Nashville Starseek Talent Show. Although unable to pursue any further recording until thirteen years later, she continued to write songs, accompanying herself on guitar and also playing locally with a Christian music group in churches, jamborees, music festivals, and for private parties and events.

Jim grew up with a passion for electronics and sound equipment, which placed him behind the scenes at many school and community performances, creating a great sound for others. He developed a great love of harmony when he became a member of the Chorus of the Onondaga Barbershop Chorus in the early eighties. It wasn't until meeting Pat that a new world of singing, writing songs, and performing opened up for him

In 2009, Pat and Jim recorded a ten-song album at Chelsea Studios in Nashville under the direction of producers Tony Migliore and Robert Metzgar. The lyrics and music on this album are drawn from emotions created from life experiences she or people close to her have had to deal with. Combined with her Christian faith, her songs reveal God as the answer to every problem from things most people experience, such as working and striving to make ends meet, to more severe problems such as depression and illness. Her wish is for the lyrics to touch listeners and give hope where hope is needed.

In 2011, the duo signed a contract with Tate Music Group from Oklahoma, who reproduced their CD under the TMG label. Their album titled "We'll Get Through" is available online at the TMG bookstore http://www.tatepublishing.com and Amazon.com as well as several other online outlets.

Pat and Jim have teamed up with guitarist, songwriter, and vocalist Paul Hutchins, also from Indian Lake, and perform their music around the Adirondack area. Currently, they are working on another recording project in the Adirondack mountain studio of Jon and Linda Hutchins, of the Boston band, "The Globs," with a goal of a 2014 release date.

Just Give My Day to Jesus

How many times have I wakened
And find my first thoughts of the day
The cleaning, the shopping, get ready for work
I wish it would all go away

I'd sit with my first cup of coffee
Listing the chores for the day
Balance the checkbook, the money's too short
Isn't that always the way
If I'd just give my day to Jesus
And let him have all that's within
I'd feel my attitude changing
As I lift up my burdens to him

Then there would be nothing to stop me
Nothing to blame as before
Time I've abused, excuses I've used
To keep me from serving the lord

Eight hours a day at my workplace
Striving to give it my best
The rest of the time there is so much to do
Until late at night when I rest

How can this all make a difference?
What possible use can I be
Then I recall, he said it all
All things are possible with me

If I'd just give my day to Jesus
And let him have all that's within
Then I'd feel my attitude changing
As I lift up my burdens to him
Then there would be nothing to stop me
Nothing to blame as before
Time I've abused, excuses I've used
To keep me from serving the lord

Now I am serving the lord

WE'LL GET THROUGH

We head out on the way in life we think things will never change
We settle in and play the hand before us that we see
But suddenly the game has changed
We'll never look at life the same
Left to navigate on new uncharted seas

It seems God has found a way to bring two souls together
Outwardly so different , but the same inside our heart and soul
We talk together, share our fears
Each others shoulders wet with tears
Seek to find direction where we need to go
We'll get through, we'll get through
We'll be there for each other as we do
We'll get through, we'll get through
And the stronger we'll be, when we do

Hey you there, sitting in the courtyard
Weren't you with the Nazarene?
Hey you there, standing at the gateway
Are you not from Galilee?
The sound of a rooster crows
The meaning of it Peter only knows
Bitter were his tears
You say you do not know this Jesus
You tell us that you're not with him
Your accent tells us that you're lying
Are you sure you're not with them?

The sound of a rooster crows
The meaning of it Peter only knows
Bitter were his tears
Simon Peter, do you truly love me?
Then feed my sheep
Simon Peter, do you truly love me?
Then feed my sheep
The third time not a sound arose
When Peter answered Lord my love you know
Then follow Me.

High Up Above

I can fly high up above as on the wings of a dove
Though the dark storm clouds that I see
Appear to be heading straight for me
I will not tremble where I stand. I trust the rock on which I stand
The fullness of peace that's in my heart
Conquers all fear of the dark

Throughout this long journey of my life I've seen both happiness and strife
No matter how wealthy I might be or if I live in poverty
We cannot measure our success by all the treasures we possess
I know that I'm rich by how I give. I know that I love by how I live

I can fly high up above as on the wings of a dove
Though the dark storm clouds that I see

Appear to be heading straight for me
I will not tremble where I stand. I trust the rock on which I stand
The fullness of peace that's in my heart
Conquers all fear of the dark

As I look down from where I soar I see the roads I took before
What I see now I could not then was how Jesus led me back to him
Although those roads I chose were wrong
It was on these that I grew strong
Lessons are learned from how we choose
But with faith in God we cannot lose

In faith we fly high up above as on the wings of a dove
Though those dark storm clouds that I see
Appear to be heading straight for me
I will not tremble where I stand. I trust the rock on which I stand
The fullness of peace that's in my heart
Conquers all fear of the dark

Locks and Chains

You say everything's all right, but as I look into your eyes
I see the smile upon your face has been placed there to disguise
The pain that's in your heart and the sadness of your soul
Is there no one you can trust to help lighten the load?

The mistakes you've made in life, Lord knows I've made my share
So I understand the guilt and shame and the feeling no one cares
I just want to let you know that these thoughts are all a lie
You've had your eyes cast down so much you passed your help right by.

So stop where you are and turn around
Lift your head and look up from the ground
Unlock the locks, loose the chains, drop that heavy load
Let the love and light of Jesus fill your soul.

The problems that you face, the sorrows that you know
Can be the masters of your life if you let them take control

I've been your road before so I could not pass you by
When I turned to the world for help it offered me a lie.

You say that there's no hope, my friend; you're very wrong
There is a way to stop the pain and to turn your cries to song
Just open up your heart let him wash your sin away
And if you want your life to change, fall on your knees and pray.

Just stop where you are and turn around, Lift your head, look up from the ground
Unlock the locks, lose the chains, and drop that heavy load
Let the love and light of Jesus fill your soul

PLEASE MOMMY PLEASE

The battle rages on outside with no chance to end
We want the choice, we have the right, we'll fight to defend
But out of sight and out of mind are not just empty words
But reality to those who have no way to be heard

Please mommy please don't listen to them
They say it's best if I come to an end
But I live and move and my heart beats within
Please mommy please don't listen to them

Deep in my world all warm and secure,
Surrounded by the gentle sounds of two beating hearts
Although beating separately the bonding's begun
I know you're my mother; I'm already your son
I know when you're happy or angry or blue
I may not understand at all, but I feel them too
When you laugh and feel glad, I feel happy too
Although you cannot see me, when you're sad, I cry too

So please, Mommy, please don't listen to them
They say it's best if I come to an end
But I live and move and my heart beats within
Please mommy please don't listen to them

Because of all these tears I cry I know something's wrong
I have not felt happiness; it seems like so long
But just a little while now, and all will be right
I will make you smile again when you hold me tight
That special time I dream about I know will not be
As the pain they said I would not feel, now hurts me
But someone's arms are waiting as my spirit takes flight
The arms of him who sent me here in love hold me tight

So please, Mommy, please don't listen to them
They say it's best if I come to an end
But I live and move and my heart beats within
Please, Mommy, please don't listen to them
Please, mommies, please don't listen to them,
Please mommies… don't listen to them

Someone Told Me

Before I knew the Lord, I lived in darkness
Surrounded by the lifestyles of the world
Trapped within the walls of greed and evil
Unable to break free from sinful will
Then I reached a point where I was beaten
The burdens were too great for me to bear
Life had let me down and death seemed welcome
How I eased that pain I did not care

"Is there a God?" I cried out in my anguish
And if there is, how could He love the likes of me?
But someone told me yes, His name is Jesus
And that someone said His name will set me free

The bitterness and fear were overwhelming

Skepticism rose inside of me
If God were real then how come He seems hidden?
I told someone, they should face reality
But somewhere deep inside I heard a whisper
Both small and quiet, at the same time loud and clear
It's said, listen to what my someone has to tell you
Just call upon my name and I will hear

"Are You there, God?" I cried out in my anguish
"And if You're there, how can You love the likes of me?"
But someone told me that Your name is Jesus
And that someone said Your name will set me free

"Yes there's a God," I cried out to my Jesus
"And now I know, that He loves the likes of me
Now I'm someone who can take the name of Jesus
And share with others, how my Savior set me free

"I'll share with others, how my Savior set me free"

The sun comes up each morning, I drag myself from bed
Stumble to the kitchen, not yet ready for the day
Will this day be different though the sun still rose the same
Will my prayers be answered ending all this pain

I lay in bed the night before, desperation in my prayers
Endless questions, how and why, what action should I take
Should I just leave well enough alone and just get by
As tears fall on my pillow blessed sleep takes me away

You can't make a heart change its mind
You can't change those feelings, so deep inside

To make others happy you have to live a lie
But you can't make a heart change its mind

No matter how I fill the day, distractions try to find
Or try to reason it away; it's always on my mind
Others say it'll be okay and God will get you through
But then they turn and walk away doing all they know to do

As long as man's been on the earth there's been the question why
From creation of the universe and how to eagles fly?
But the only thing I'd ever want is an answer to this
How does one find peace when mind and feelings contradict?

'Cause you can't make a heart change its mind, you can't change those feelings, so deep inside,
To keep others happy, you have to live a lie
But you can't make a heart change its mind.

When The Trumpet Sounds

He's the Lord of all creation. He's my cause for celebration
In the midst of tribulation, I will praise his name
I'll praise him from the housetops; from the highest peaks I won't stop
With my eyes upturned, I'll keep watch for the coming of the king

When the trumpet sounds, I will head to glory
I'll be heaven bound, where my lord will surely meet me
In the clouds my eternal family
Will be there when the trumpet sounds

We have a work to do here and as I strive I won't fear
I feel his holy spirit near me with me all the way
I'll always keep an open ear at time when I am feeling weary
In the hopes I soon will hear it on that blessed day

Oh, when the trumpet sounds I will head to glory
I'll be heaven bound, where my lord will surely meet me
In the clouds my eternal family will be there when the trumpet sounds

THE WINDS THAT BLOW

We live our lives from day to day, from well-laid plans, we dare not stray
To realize our hopes and dreams is the goal to gain
The calendar marks off the years, the clock the seconds, minutes, hours
Like actors in an endless play our script remains unchanged

We think we have it in control when everything just seems to flow
The pieces fit together as deception works its charm
When everything be gins to shake is when we notice our mistake
Helplessly, we watch as all we live for tumbles down

Complacency had infiltrated, routine had been tolerated
Not so much in darkness as unwillingness to know
Then all our dreams come crashing down, the walls we built no longer sound
Only then we'll see we're subject to the winds that blow

When the comfort zones no longer there the elements begin to tear
Away the bits of fabric from our hearts our minds our souls
After all the winds have blown, we stand exposed and all we own
Are tears upon our cheeks and in Gods hand a broken heart

But in his hand new life will start as only with a contrite heart
Can God command that miracle of healing to begin?
The mighty winds that broke the calm have now become our healing balm
When we finally put our trust in to the masters plan

Complacency had infiltrated, routine had been tolerated
Not so much in darkness as unwillingness to know
Then all our dreams come crashing down, the walls we built no longer sound
Only then we'll see we're subject to the winds that blow

Photographer Biography

Paul Gana started photographing Colorado's landscapes as a means of documenting his climbs of the state's many majestic mountains. Over time he realized that the state's scenery was worth sharing. What a more perfect place than Colorado can there be? A quote from his website Paulscoloradophotography.com states "I have heard Colorado being referred to as 'Gods Country', and in the words of the great Teddy Roosevelt when on a tour of this state referred to it as a place that 'bankrupts the English language'! I couldn't agree more."

Most of his photographic skills were developed by trial and error ("Mostly error," Paul says with a laugh). He read as many books on photography as he could and sought answers and advice from fellow photographers to be able to capture magnificent images with his own unique perspective. Paul has had several gallery exhibits, currently and quite regularly at the Denver Photo Art gallery, which is part of John Fielder's Colorado, owned by renowned nature photographer John Fielder. He is always looking for more opportunities for gallery showings.

listen|imagine|view|experience

WE'll GET THROUGH SONG DOWNLOAD INCLUDED WITH THIS BOOK!

In your hands you hold a complete digital entertainment package. In addition to the paper version, you receive a free download of the audio version of this book. Simply use the code listed below when visiting our website. Once downloaded to your computer, you can listen to the book through your computer's speakers, burn it to an audio CD or save the file to your portable music device (such as Apple's popular iPod) and listen on the go!

How to get your free song download:

1. Visit www.tatepublishing.com and click on the e|LIVE logo on the home page.
2. Enter the following coupon code:
    063a-0dbc-e393-4fdc-8434-925e-486d-cea5
3. Download the song from your e|LIVE digital locker and begin enjoying your new digital entertain-
    ment package today!